Memorial Day
E Holiday   149318

Wilton Public Library

CCS			
WDC			

DEMCO

MEMORIAL DAY

BY TRUDI STRAIN TRUEIT · ILLUSTRATED BY RONNIE ROONEY

Published in the United States of America by The Child's World®
1980 Lookout Drive • Mankato, MN 56003-1705
800-599-READ • www.childsworld.com

ACKNOWLEDGMENTS
The Child's World®: Mary Berendes, Publishing Director

The Design Lab: Kathleen Petelinsek, Design; Julia Goozen, Page Production

Editorial Direction: Red Line Editorial, Patricia Stockland, Managing Editor

LIBRARY OF CONGRESS CATALOGING-IN-PUBLICATION DATA
Trueit, Trudi Strain.
  Memorial Day / by Trudi Strain Trueit ; illustrated by Ronnie Rooney.
    p. cm. — (Holidays, festivals & celebrations)
  Includes bibliographical references and index.
  Audience: Grades K-3.
  ISBN-13: 978-1-59296-815-2 (library bound : alk. paper)
  ISBN-10: 1-59296-815-5 (library bound : alk. paper)
  1. Memorial Day—Juvenile literature. I. Rooney, Ronnie. II. Title.

E642.T78 2007
394.262—dc22   2006103390

TABLE OF CONTENTS

CHAPTER ONE

SOME GAVE ALL

"The United States and the freedom for which it stands, the freedom for which they died, must endure and prosper. Their lives remind us that freedom is not bought cheaply. It has a cost; it imposes a burden."
—Ronald Reagan (1911–2004), Memorial Day speech, 1982

Row after row of small U.S. flags stretch across a cemetery. Each one stands next to the grave of an American soldier. People walk quietly among the flags. Some stop to lay flowers on the gravestones.

Today is the last Monday in May. It is Memorial Day in the United States.

A memorial is a lasting tribute. It helps us to remember an important person, group, or event in history.

Memorial Day was created to honor the brave people who were killed fighting in U.S. wars. It is the nation's promise that those who died in the line of duty will never be forgotten.

People visit cemeteries on Memorial Day.

CHAPTER TWO

A NATION DIVIDED

Union soldiers were from the North. They wore blue uniforms.

Confederate soldiers were from the South. They wore gray uniforms.

In the mid-1800s, slavery was tearing the United States apart. Southern states felt slavery should be legal. The North disagreed. Many states in the South went so far as to form a new country, called the Confederate States of America. This led to the Civil War (1861–1865).

Friends and family from different parts of the United States often found themselves on opposite sides of the war. Sometimes, they had to fight each other—brother against brother, father against son.

In these sad times, women in the South began decorating the graves of southern Confederate soldiers with flowers. They decorated the graves of northern Union soldiers, too.

In 1865, the North finally won the war. The United States remained a single nation! Even so, it was hard for those in the North to celebrate. More than 600,000 soldiers had been killed. Never before or since then have so many Americans died in one war.

Many soldiers were killed in battle during the U.S. Civil War.

"What a cruel thing is war: to separate and destroy families and friends, and mar the purest joys and happiness God has granted us in this world; to fill our hearts with hatred instead of love for our neighbors, and to devastate the fair face of this beautiful world."
—Robert E. Lee (1807–1870), Confederate General

CHAPTER THREE

DECORATION DAY

"That we here highly resolve that these dead shall not have died in vain; that this nation, under God, shall have a new birth of freedom; and that government, by the people, for the people, shall not perish from the earth."
—Abraham Lincoln (1809–1865), Gettysburg Address, 1863

After the Civil War, Americans looked for a special way to honor their fallen war heroes. Military leaders remembered how southern women had decorated the graves of soldiers on both sides.

In the spring of 1868, Union General John Alexander Logan declared that each May 30th would be a day to remember those who had died in the Civil War. He called it Decoration Day.

The first national celebration was held at Arlington National Cemetery in Virginia. Arlington is a military cemetery near Washington, D.C.

President Abraham Lincoln wanted the nation to remember those who had lost their lives in the Civil War.

On November 19, 1863, President Abraham Lincoln gave a speech at Gettysburg, Pennsylvania. He was there as part of a dedication to the new Soldiers Cemetery. The ceremony honored those who had died in the Civil War battles there that summer. Today, the place is called Gettysburg National Cemetery. Both the cemetery and Lincoln's speech are now famous tributes to the fallen soldiers.

People placed flowers on the graves of thousands of Union and Confederate soldiers. They gave speeches and sang patriotic songs.

By the 1890s, Decoration Day was more commonly known as Memorial Day.

After the Civil War, people began decorating soldiers' graves with flowers.

"The 30th of May, 1868, is designated for the purpose of strewing with flowers, or otherwise decorating the graves of comrades who died in defense of their country during the late rebellion, and whose bodies now lie in almost every city, village, and hamlet church-yard in the land."
—John A. Logan (1826–1886)

CHAPTER FOUR

FLOWERS FOR THE FALLEN

During World War I (1914–1918), thousands of U.S. soldiers died on the battlefields of Europe. Often, the first wildflowers to sprout on a field after a battle were poppies. The bright red flowers soon became a symbol for fallen soldiers.

In 1918, a teacher from Georgia named Moina Michael read a poem about the poppy fields. She decided to wear a silk poppy on Memorial Day to pay tribute to Americans killed in the war. Moina began making and selling poppies. She donated the money to veterans groups.

After World War I, Memorial Day was expanded to honor all Americans in the armed forces who died in wartime. In 1971, the U.S. Congress made Memorial Day a national holiday. It was moved to the last Monday in May.

Wearing a poppy on Memorial Day shows respect for the armed forces.

Over time, Moina Michael's poppy sales raised more than $200 million for veterans groups in the United States and England. In 1948, the U.S. Post Office honored her by putting her portrait on a stamp!

CHAPTER FIVE

CELEBRATING MEMORIAL DAY

On Memorial Day, every ship in the U.S. Navy and all naval stations fire a twenty-one gun salute at noon.

Many Americans visit a cemetery or war monument on Memorial Day. They may attend a ceremony where veterans speak, a band plays, and the military fires a twenty-one gun salute. Boom!

Each year, thousands of people travel to Arlington National Cemetery. They listen to the president of the United States give a speech. The president also lays a wreath at the Tomb of the Unknowns.

The Tomb of the Unknowns holds the remains of several unidentified American soldiers from different wars. They represent all Americans who died for their country. A soldier always guards the tomb, always.

In 2000, the U.S. Congress created a National Moment of Remembrance on Memorial Day. At 3 P.M. on the holiday, Americans are asked to stop what they are doing to remember the nation's fallen soldiers. In this moment of silence, what will you think about?

The Tomb of the Unknowns is guarded day and night, all year round.

"They defended our nation, they liberated the oppressed, they served the cause of peace. And all Americans who have known the loss and sadness of war, whether recently or long ago, can know this: The person they love and miss is honored and remembered by the United States of America."
—George W. Bush
  (1946–present),
  Memorial Day
  Address, 2004

CHAPTER SIX

THE COLORS OF THE UNITED STATES FLAG:

White stands for purity and innocence.

Red stands for valor and hardiness.

Blue stands for vigilance, perseverance, and justice.

STARS AND STRIPES FOREVER

The U.S. flag is an important part of Memorial Day.

It is tradition to lower the flag to half-staff until noon on the holiday as a sign of respect. People wave flags during Memorial Day parades, speeches, and concerts. Scout troops, military groups, and citizens place small flags on the graves of American soldiers.

Did you know that there are more than 300,000 military graves at Arlington National Cemetery? Each one gets its own flag! It is a custom called flags-in. Soldiers from the 3rd U.S. Infantry place the flags in the ground. They keep a 24-hour watch during the weekend before Memorial Day to make sure none of the flags fall.

Why do they do this? Because throughout history, more than one million men and women have died protecting the freedoms, land, and people for which the U.S. flag stands.

Flags-in honors fallen soldiers.

The 3rd U.S. Infantry is also known as The Old Guard, and for good reason. It's the oldest active-duty unit in the Army. The Old Guard got its start back in 1784!

"I only regret that I have but one life to lose for my country."
—Nathan Hale
(1755–1776),
American patriot

CHAPTER SEVEN

POETRY CORNER

The Blue and The Gray

By the flow of the inland river,
Whence the fleets of iron have fled,
Where the blades of the grave-grass quiver,
Asleep on the ranks of the dead;
Under the sod and the dew,
Waiting the judgment day;
Under the one, the Blue;
Under the other, the Gray.
—Francis Miles Finch (1827–1907)

"To preserve the peace, we must never forget the sacrifices that have paved the way to peace."
—Bill Clinton, Memorial Day Address, 2000

In Flanders Fields

In Flanders fields the poppies blow
Between the crosses, row on row,
That mark our place; and in the sky
The larks, still bravely singing, fly
Scarce heard amid the guns below.
We are the Dead. Short days ago
We lived, felt dawn, saw sunset glow,
Loved and were loved, and now we lie
In Flanders fields.

Take up our quarrel with the foe:
To you from failing hands we throw
The torch: be yours to hold it high.
If ye break faith with us who die
We shall not sleep, though poppies grow
In Flanders fields.
—John McCrae (1872–1918),
* Canadian doctor*

The poem "In Flanders Fields" remembers the soldiers who died in World War I. Moina Michael's idea for silk poppies came from the poppies mentioned in this poem.

We Shall Keep the Faith

Oh! You who sleep in Flanders Fields,
Sleep sweet-to rise anew!
We caught the torch you threw
And holding high, we keep the Faith
With all who died.
We cherish, too, the poppy red
That grows on fields where valor led;
It seems to signal to the skies
That blood of heroes never dies,
But lends a lustre to the red
Of the flower that blooms above the dead
In Flanders Fields.
—Moina Michael (1869–1944)

CHAPTER EIGHT

SONGS OF MEMORIAL DAY

Battle Hymn of the Republic

Mine eyes have seen the glory of the coming of the Lord:
He is trampling out the vintage where the grapes of
      wrath are stored;
He hath loosed the fateful lightning of His terrible swift
      sword:
His truth is marching on.

Chorus:
Glory, glory, hallelujah,
Glory, glory, hallelujah,
Glory, glory, hallelujah,
His truth is marching on.
—words by Julia Ward Howe (1819–1910)

"The Battle Hymn of the Republic" is often sung on Memorial Day. Julia Ward Howe wrote the words to the song while visiting the Capitol during the Civil War.

Taps

Fading light dims the sight,
And a star gems the sky, gleaming bright.
From afar drawing nigh falls the night.
Day is done, gone the sun,
From the lake, from the hills, from the sky.
All is well, safely rest, God is nigh.
—words and music by Major General
  Daniel Butterfield (1831–1901)

"Taps" is usually played on a bugle or trumpet. It is the traditional music used at funerals honoring soldiers.

Star-Spangled Banner

Oh, say can you see, by the dawn's early light
What so proudly we hailed at the twilight's last gleaming?
Whose broad stripes and bright stars through the perilous fight,
O'er the ramparts we watched were so gallantly streaming?
And the rocket's red glare, the bombs bursting in air,
Gave proof through the night that our flag was still there.
Oh, say does that star-spangled banner yet wave
O'er the land of the free and the home of the brave?
—words by Francis Scott Key (1779–1843)

Francis Scott Key wrote the words to the "Star-Spangled Banner" in 1814. The poem celebrated American victory over the British in the War of 1812. It did not become the national anthem until 1931.

Joining in the Spirit of Memorial Day

- Do you have any relatives or ancestors who died in the line of duty? If so, interview family members and search through scrap books and photo albums to find out more about these people.

- Visit a cemetery where soldiers are buried. Look for graves that have not been decorated. Place flowers or flags next to them to pay your respects.

- Do you have a parent or grandparent that is a veteran? Ask them about their wartime experiences. How do they celebrate the holiday?

- Spend Memorial Day visiting a local or national war monument. Learn about the war it represents and the people who gave their lives in battle.

- On Memorial Day, remember to pause for a moment of silence at 3 P.M. to honor fallen soldiers.

- Attend a Memorial Day service, parade, or concert.

- Wear a poppy! Get your friends to wear one, too.

Making a Patriotic Float

What you need:

Red soda, in any flavor (strawberry or raspberry work well)
Vanilla ice cream or frozen yogurt
Blueberries

Strawberries
Whipped cream topping
A tall glass
An ice cream spoon

Directions:

Put one scoop of the ice cream into the glass. Fill the glass with red soda until it is almost full, letting the ice cream float on top. Put some whipped cream topping on top of the floating ice cream. Decorate the very top with blueberries and a strawberry. Enjoy the tasty red, white, and blue!

Making Poppies to Wear

What you need:

Pencil
Red and black construction paper
Scissors
Glue
Green pipe cleaners

Directions:

Draw a 2-inch circle on the red paper. Draw a smaller circle on the black paper. Cut out both circles and glue the small black circle to the top of the red circle.

Tie one end of a green pipe cleaner into a small knot. Take the other end of the pipe cleaner and poke it through the center of the black circle. Pull the pipe cleaner all the way through the circles until just the knot is on the black side. The long part of the pipe cleaner should be out through the red side. The knot is the center of the flower, and the long part is the stem.

Be sure to make poppies for your friends and family, too!

Words to Know

half-staff—the point halfway up a flagpole

monument—a statue, building, or site that pays tribute to a person, group, or event

patriotic—showing love for one's country

slavery—a system where people are forced to work for others

symbol—an object that stands for an idea

tradition—a long-held custom

twenty-one gun salute—a military honor where twenty-one shots are fired from a rifle, cannon, or other firearm

veterans—people who have served in the armed forces

How to Learn More about Memorial Day

At the Library

Cotton, Jacqueline. *Memorial Day*. New York, NY: Children's
   Press, 2002.

Haugen, David (editor). *Soldiers*. San Diego, CA: Blackbirch
   Press, 2004.

Ross, Kathy. *Star Spangled Crafts*. Brookfield CT: Millbrook
   Press, 2003.

Schaefer, Ted. *Arlington National Cemetery*. Chicago, IL:
   Heinemann Library, 2006.

Schomp, Virginia. *World War I*. New York, NY: Marshall
   Cavendish, 2004.

On the Web

Visit our Web site for lots of links about Memorial Day:
http://www.childsworld.com/links
NOTE TO PARENTS, TEACHERS, AND LIBRARIANS:
We routinely verify our Web links to make sure they're safe,
active sites—so encourage your readers to check them out!

ABOUT THE AUTHOR

Trudi Strain Trueit is a former television news reporter and anchor. She has written more than forty books for children. She lives in Everett, Washington, with her husband, Bill, a teacher.

ABOUT THE ILLUSTRATOR

Ronnie Rooney grew up on the south shore of Massachusetts. Her first love has always been art, followed closely by the ocean, dogs, and the United States of America.

Index